26 Things That Bug Me

By Michael Raupp

With drawings by Jeff Kollins

International Society of Arboriculture

The first edition of *26 Things That Bug Me* was published by Barclay Bryan Press, Inc.
© 2010 Michael Raupp and Jeff Kollins

second edition

All photographs are courtesy of the author.
Illustrations: Jeff Kollins
Book Design and Layout: Samuel Copeland
Editorial and Production Manager: Amy Theobald

International Society of Arboriculture

International Society of Arboriculture
Champaign, Illinois, U.S.
+1.217.355.9411
permissions@isa-arbor.com
www.isa-arbor.com

Printed by Martin One Source, Champaign, Illinois, U.S.

10 9 8 7 6 5 4

1019-CA-500

ISBN: 978-1-881956-83-9

To George, Hilda, Ivan, Deak, Hank, and Bon for telling me stories

To Michael, Erin, Brian, and Paula for listening to my stories

To Sharon, Tina, Linda, Ethel, and Sheri for bringing out this story

To all my friends in print, radio, and television who help me share bug stories with people

HELLO!

My name is Mantie, and how do you do?
I'd like to practice some letters with you!
Just turn the pages and look carefully.
If you are lucky, you might just find me!

A is for Antlion

The antlion sits in a deep, sandy pit.

She catches small bugs tumbling down inside it.

Small ants, tiny beetles, she finds them all yummy!

A snippity snap, and they're safe in her tummy.

B is for Bumble Bee

The bumble bee bumbles from flower to flower,

Sipping sweet nectar in each waking hour.

The nectar and pollen go straight to her hive

To feed her bee babies and keep them alive.

C is for Cicada

For seventeen years, they are not to be found.

They are sucking on plant roots down deep underground!

To the treetops they fly after waiting so long,

And they sing to each other their wonderful song.

D is for Dragonfly

Dragonflies dance in the blue summer skies,

With powerful wings and two great big eyes.

They swoop through the air catching bugs on the wing

And eat while they zoom. They are cool. That's their thing.

E is for Earwig

The earwig, my dear, is nothing to fear.

Despite what you heard, it won't climb in your ear.

Those pinchers you see at the end of its tail

Are for picking up groceries, garbage, and mail.

F is for Firefly

Fireflies are great bugs to catch in a jar
On a dark summer night, when they blink like a star.
If you catch one, remember, you should set it free.
They must eat, rest, and play just like you and like me.

G is for Green Lacewing

Look closely—these lacewings are beautiful things,
With shiny green eyes and delicate wings.
But small lacewing youngsters do not give out hugs.
They are hungry meat eaters and eat other bugs!

H is for Hickory Horned Devil

The horns on this devil are easy to see
As it gobbles the leaves of a hickory tree.
This big caterpillar should cause you no fear.
It becomes a large moth in less than a year.

I is for Ixodes

Look out for Ixodes the black-legged tick.

If this one should bite you, it could make you sick.

When you come inside, carefully look all about.

If you find any ticks, pick them off, toss them out.

J is for Japanese Beetle

These beetles feast in the month of July.

You see them on plants where they run, walk, and fly.

They like to eat roses and all kinds of leaves.

Their babies, called grubs, munch on roots as they please.

K is for Katydid

Katy did, katy didn't is what these insects say.
The guys sing at night but not during the day.
They make their weird bug songs by rubbing their wings.
They hear with their legs! Oh my! What strange things!

L is for Ladybug

These ladies are good bugs to have on your plants.

They eat pesty bugs. They don't give them a chance.

So, bad bugs watch out! You better be ready,

Or you will disappear like a plate of spaghetti.

M is for Monarch Butterfly

The monarch is queen of the butterfly clan.

When young, she eats milkweeds. It's part of her plan.

The fall is the season she favors the best.

She flies to the south for some sun and a rest.

N is for Nymph

Nymph is the name for a very young bug.

If they were way big, you could give them a hug.

As nymphs grow and change, they do very strange things—

Like turn into adults with two pairs of wings.

O is for Opilionid

You might know these critters as Daddy-Long-Legs.
The dads don't do much but the moms lay the eggs.
With plenty of legs they stroll through the land,
And make awful smells with their stinky stink gland.

P is for Praying Mantid

Oh, I am fantastic at catching my prey!

Cricket is on the lunch menu today.

Two spiny legs help me capture my food.

I eat the head first to avoid being rude.

 is for Queen Butterfly

The queen butterfly has some tricky surprises.

She basks in the sun as soon as it rises,

And if birdies catch her, she has a good trick.

One taste of her blood makes them throw up! How sick!

R is for Robber Fly

The robber fly's face is remarkably hairy.

To many small bugs he looks really quite scary!

When no one is watching, the robber will pounce

And eat tiny bugs by the gram or the ounce.

S is for Saddleback Caterpillar

The saddleback dresses in brown and light green.
But don't let that fool you, this babe can be mean!
The spiny spines found on the head and the tail
Sting badly enough to make grown-up men wail.

T is for Tiger Beetle

This tiger can't growl. He can't snarl, yell, or roar.

But he runs, jumps, and hides on the dark forest floor.

If you try to catch him, you better be quick

And have a big net on a bug-catching stick.

U is for Unicorn Beetle

Unicorn beetles have really great horns!

They look just like crazy enormous-sized thorns.

The boy beetles use them for fighting, you see.

They battle for places to live in a tree.

V is for Velvet Ant

Do not let the velvet ant get in your pants!

If she does, you'll be dancing the velvet ant dance.

She can give you a sting. She can give you a bite.

You will hop, skip, and jump on one leg half the night!

W is for Wheel Bug

The wheel bug wears giant spokes on her back.

She moves very *s l o w* as she plans an attack!

The large beak you see in between her front legs

Is for poking and eating small bugs and their eggs.

X is for Xylocopa Bee

Xylocopa is really a carpenter bee.

The work of the mom is quite something to see.

Her jaws carve a perfectly round hole in wood

To serve as a home for her babes. She is good!

Y is for Yellow Jacket

This fierce fancy lady is easy to see.

Her cheek is bright yellow and so is her knee.

She lives with her mom in a papery nest.

Applesauce is one of the foods she likes best.

Z is for Zebra Butterfly

How did this butterfly get its cool name?

It looks like a zebra! The stripes are the same.

If you want to know where this mom's babies might be,

Just look on the leaves of the strange paw paw tree.

Wasn't it fun meeting my friends and me?
Did you learn every bug and each ABC?
If not, have no worries, for here's a good plan.
Just open your book and read it again.

When you finish, be sure to jump up, run, and play.
Go outside. Look for lots of cool bugs right away.
Learn all of their names and observe what they do.
And see if some bugs are like me and like you.

So long! For now, Mantie bids you adieu.
Next time we meet, I'll bring more friends for you.

Mantie and Mike

Mike Raupp is a Professor of Entomology. He studies insects and enjoys them every day. He often shares his stories about insects on television and radio and tells people about cool things insects do. He likes to go outside on safaris and take pictures of insects doing strange, funny things. He loves telling bug stories to make people laugh.

Jeff Kollins is an artist who lives in a little brick house with his beautiful wife and amazing daughter. He loves to draw magical places, cool creatures, and other fantastically fun stuff. When he isn't busy with paint brushes, Jeff enjoys curling up with a good book—especially one with pictures.